EAST COAST LIMERICKS

By the Readers of
Atlantic Insight

Collected and Edited by George Peabody

Formac Publishing Company Limited
1989

Cover Design: Kevin O'Reilly
Cover illustration by: Robert Williams
Illustrations by: Robert Williams

Canadian Cataloguing in Publication Data

Main entry under title:
East Coast Limericks
   ISBN 0-88780-075-0
1. Limericks.   I. Peabody, George.
PS8285.LSE37 1989   C811' .O7508'9711   C89-098682-7
PR9195.85.L5E37 1989

Published with the assistance of the Nova Scotia Department of Tourism and Culture

An Atlantic Insight Book

Formac Publishing Company Limited
5502 Atlantic Street
Halifax, Nova Scotia
B3H 1G6

Printed and bound in Canada.

INTRODUCTION

As forms of verse go, the limerick has a short history and a disreputable image. The mere mention of limericks dredges up from our memories vague recollections of young ladies named Jude, old men from Nantucket, and mathematicians who lived in Bengal. Limericks of this sort, though the common contemporary fare, would have mortified the respectable though eccentric Victorian artist credited with starting it all.

Edward Lear may not have invented the limerick— the *Oxford Companion to English Literature* suggests that the form originated as a country house parlour game early in the nineteenth century, presumably in the Irish county of the same name—but he brought it to a general audience. Lear was a rhymester of talent who is most remembered today as the author of *The Owl and the Pussycat*. He also gave art lessons to Queen Victoria, and probably composed limericks and other "nonsense verse" for the royal children.

Lear's limericks had all the essentials which have marked the form ever since: the rhythm, the *aabba* rhyme pattern, and the whimsy and wit of all successful examples. They did have two major differences to contemporary limericks: they were rarely ribald, scatalogical or obscene, and the final line was often a repetition or near repetition of the initial line.

Like many people, I first encountered the limerick in junior high school—though not in English class. I no longer recall the specific example, but I'm pretty sure it wasn't one which Edward Lear would have acknowledged. Ever since that initial exposure, though, I have been an admirer of comic verse. In high school I tried composing limericks; fortunately, these have vanished into the more obscure recesses of my memory (and have, I hope, passed totally beyond the recollection of anyone else!)

My career as an occasional limerickist really began in the early 1970s while I was working on an alternate newspaper in Vancouver. One day a co-worker drew my attention to a peculiar classified ad:

> *Anglican vicar in want*
> *of a second-hand portable font.*
> *Will accept for the same*
> *a portrait in frame*
> *of the Bishop-elect of Vermont.*

As an old limerick fan, I recognized a classic of the genre—and I also noted in passing that whoever had submitted it had, perhaps inadvertantly, substituted "accept" for the proper "trade," thus destroying the internal logic of the thing. It was a slow afternoon so I composed the following for the next week's classified ads:

> *Clerical persons who seek*
> *odd objects in ads every week*
> *might like to choose*
> *from a shipment of pews,*
> *all new, all made out of teak.*

This brought an irate response in the form of a letter from someone signing himself "The Vicar of the Parish of St. Norman," upbraiding me for injecting a note of sordid commercialism into what he had intended as a harmless clerical jest. I considered this somewhat suspect—I had never heard of a Saint Norman and could find no such church in the Vancouver directory. Accordingly, I exercised my editorial privilege and appended these limericks when we printed his letter:

> *The Vicar,*
> *St. Norman's Manse,*
> *Sir:*
> *To dignify you with an answer,*
> *It behooves me to note*
> *Your original quote*
> *Was flawed.*
> *I remain,*
> *Yours,*
> *A Fan, sir.*
>
> *And just by way of postscript,*
> *Might I say that I find you loose-lipped!*
> *If you don't want my pews*
> *You don't have to choose.*
> *Go lock thyself in thy crypt!*

That closed the exchange. I have never been entirely certain whether I was dealing with a genuine man of the cloth or not, but I later came to suspect it was a Vancouver writer who published a couple of satirical novels under the pseudonym Vicar Vicars.

I will restrain myself and not perpetuate in print any of my subsequent limericks except for one I wrote in the mid-1980s for Elizabeth May, the environmental activist, who was then articling as a lawyer in Halifax. There had been a number of "political" legal cases around that time, and there was a general feeling that the Nova Scotia judiciary was not perhaps of the highest quality (an impression which some more recent cases have done little to contradict.)

> *The judges in Halifax courts*
> *Are easily put out of sorts.*
> > *Their procedures are crude,*
> > *They're dyspeptic and rude*
> *And they don't know their writs from their torts.*

I say little of more recent exploits like the exchange in the classified ad column of the Woodstock *Bugle* in early 1988 which so mystified some readers that I received several curious and obscure letters in reply including one which I think was a proposal of marriage from a bachelor who had made a mistake in my gender. It was certainly a proposal of something...

I would be lying if I said this book had a serious purpose. I suggested it to the publisher because I thought it would be fun to do. I hope it will also be fun to read. If there's a point to it beyond that (aside from the millions and millions of dollars I expect to make in royalties, of course), it is in encouraging people who are not Poets to write poetry. In this region—and probably in other parts of the country as well—there are thousands of people who like to write verse. They do it for their own enjoyment and to entertain their friends and family. They write poems to mark occasions at work, in the family and in their communities. Few of them make it into any form of print other than the photocopier.

Hardly anyone in the "poetry establishment" takes the work of these community poets seriously. Their poems are usually described as doggerel or ignored entirely. And many of the verses *are* badly made, the sentiments *are* trite, the images *are* banal. But this is not true of all of timents *are* trite, the images *are* banal. But this is not true of all of them. Some, like many of the limericks in this collection, are well-crafted examples of light verse written by people who have a talent for expressing themselves this way. They should be encouraged, and their work should receive wider circulation.

Many of the limericks in this book were entries in the *Great Atlantic Canada Limerick Contest* which *Atlantic Insight* magazine ran as part of its 10th Anniversary celebrations. For the ad which told readers about the contest, I whipped off the following limerick:

> *If you have a flair for light verse,*
> *And can keep your verbosity terse,*
>   *Get your muse to perform*
>   *In the limerick form*
> *And write us one better—or worse!*

It was, intentionally, a pretty lame limerick: designed to inspire readers to say "Well, hell, if *that's* their standard, then even I can write a better one than that!" I did not take into consideration a certain strain of literal-mindedness that exists in *Atlantic Insight* readers. The final two words of my limerick were not intended as a challenge; they were there for the rhyme, that's all. Unfortunately some readers took up the unintended challenge; some carried it so far as to submit entries which were not even limericks, were in *vers libre*, did not rhyme or were in prose form.

Fortunately, most readers did get the right idea.

As well as entries in the *Insight* contest, this collection contains a number of limericks solicited especially for publication here—and, since I could not reasonably expect others to do what I was not willing to do myself, some which I have written for the book.

The *Grand Prize* winner in the *Insight* contest stood

and shoulders above them, though some might consider this a pun.) In addition to its poetic prominence, it used three of my favourite New Brunswick place names as rhyming words, and had the further distinction of being modestly risqué (if that's not a contradiction in terms!).

> *A tough guy from Tabusintac*
> *Ate some dynamite sticks for a snack.*
> > *They found part of his liver*
> > *In Bartibog River,*
> *And his rectum in Kouchibouguac!*
> > > — *George Sutherland*

Contents

POLITICAL

**Some of the limericks were
explicitly political**

A matronly Tory named Dawn
Said, "You'll never believe where I've gone!
    The party chose me
    To go out to tea
And hobnob with Mavis and John!"
                            —*Judy Paul*

An N.B. politician once said
"I know Ottawa's in the red,
    But if they had any brains,
    They'd leave us our trains
And cut AECL instead."
                            —*Joe MacIntosh*

There once was a man named Trudeau
Who brought in an era nouveau,
    He taught "Just Society"
    With dignity and piety,
But never told us it was Just-for-him, though!
                            —*John D. Thurber*

"That bridge will act like a drain,"
The Island storeowners complain.
    "Our consumers will flee:
    They'll all drive to N.B.
And shop at the Mall de Champlain."
                    —*T. Ferguson*

Whose idea is it to think
That P.E.I. needs a fixed link?
    Someone from away
    Always gets the last say
On whether *we* should swim or sink.
                    —*Mary McInnis*

Said the premier known as Frank
"On this my mind is a blank:
  It's a curious position
  Having no Opposition,
But who do you think I should thank?"
                    —*Michael Allen*

The former Preem of N.B.
Said "All right! It was me!
  But how could I say,
  On that particular day,
I was just holding it for Her Majesty?"
                    —*Paul Cyr*

Said Moncton's mayor with a frown,
"This city's a company town —
  We'll raise a helluva fuss:
  What'll happen to us
If CN just shuts the shops down?"
                    —*P. Steeves*

Those Bluenose politicians aren't dumb:
They know from where their votes come.
   To voters who travel,
   They give loads of gravel;
Still others get mickeys of rum.
                     —*J.K. Anderson*

A Cole Harbour man, city bound,
By a bridge committee was found.
    One-half million, no less
    Won him the contest.
Now he's happy he lived out of town!
                    —*Dave Hingley*

Let's all hope the vote's fairly tossed
How Islanders go straight across —
    The tide turns on the brink,
    Should it flow with a link?
Does a stony road gather no moss?
                    —*Jim Benjamin*

McKenna says government's tough,
With no foes, it's really been rough.
    All those poor MLA's,
    Not knowing their place,
And no one to call out their bluff.
                    —*Alex Merrill*

An overwhelming response from
Newfoundland created a special "Sprung"
sub-category.

There was a young premier named Brian,
On Sprung he was surely relyin'.
     The cukes they all failed.
     Our Brian, he wailed,
Now he's "flyin'" and "cryin'" and "sighin'."
                              —*Jacqueline Barrett*

There once was a premier named Brian
Who said, "By God, I'll keep tryin'
     To grow something at Sprung,
     Even beach rocks or dung
Despite all this sabotage and spyin'."
                              —*Jeanette Winsor*

A scheme of the lucrative kind
Sprung to life in the Premier's mind,
     Died, and Peckford retired
     When the cukes all expired,
Leaving only a lemon behind.
                              —*M.I. Young*

We're all in a glow in St. John's;
Our shades we have to keep drawn.
Double Daylight Time
And Sprung greenhouse shine
Give us daytime from dusk until dawn.
—M. Knott

From Alberta's climate so cold
Came a legend, daring and bold:
   "There's gold in cucumbers
   When grown in large numbers
But only if government bank-rolled."
                    —*Lorne Ramsay*

Our government's truly unique —
They built a bridge over a creek
   With no roads leading to it.
   Ask "Why did they do it?" —
They'll call it the Buchanan Mystique
                    —*M. Weagle*

Sysco's a fiscal cesspool;
The way it eats dollars is cruel.
   More millions each year
   (And billions, we fear):
Are they burning it all up as fuel?
                    —*David Perry*

(New Brunswick's proposed bunker is
designed with plate glass windows)

Debert has a bunker or two,
Undergound, to shelter a few
    In a nuclear war.
    And they're building one more
In New Brunswick, complete with a view!
              —*Liz Andrews*

We have John and Alexa and Vince,
Who all did their best to convince
    Us to vote the right way
    Last election day,
But we haven't heard much from them since.
              —*Mildred Burrows*

LIMERICKS OF SOCIAL COMMENT

There's a house that I often drive by,
Which is loved by the large butterfly.
    On the walls rest a score;
    On the shed even more:
Some call it a sore for the eye!
              —*Peter MacLean*

A South Shore artist named Ron
Has a statue of Bambi the fawn
    Made of used polyesters,
    Along with fourteen Sylvesters,
And Tweetie-birds out out on his lawn!
              —*J.K. Anderson*

A potato farmer who felt growing pains
Thought, "I'll have *such* a crop if it rains,
    I can sell at a bounty,
    Buy up half the county,
And control as much land as McCains!"
              —*Peter DeMerchant*

A park warden at Kouchibouguac,
Said "Yes, I *was* taken aback
    When the staff ran to me
    Yelling 'Quick! Come and see!
It's Jackie Vautour! He's come back!'"
          —*George Peabody*

We who in New Brunswick do dwell
Know a word that's more scary than Hell.
    We don't speak it aloud
    Except in a crowd:
It's the "I-word": that's all I dare tell.
                    —*Susan Saunders*

We're moving from Uniacke Square
To only the Housing knows where.
    Not Spryfield, I pray:
    It'll take half the day
To get back downtown from out there.
                    —*M. Carter*

A Halifax magazine titled *Frank*
Published gossip both scurrilous and rank.
    "It's all very witty,"
    Said the owners, "Tough titty!"
And laughed all the way to their bank.
                    —*A.S. Brown*

At Georgetown on Cardigan Bay,
The fish live indoors, so they say.
   There's roomsful of trout,
   But pessimists doubt
That the owners can make the thing pay.
—*George Peabody*

A sullen and sinking sand dollar
Said, "Here's a notion to flounder a scholar —
    A funny notation,
    This thing called inflation:
It don't make me bigger, but smaller!"
                    —*Jim Benjamin*

Before I arrived in this town
Chocolate I always turned down.
    Now I'm faced with Ganong
    And no matter how strong,
In sweets, I could easily drown.
                    —*Alex Merrill*

(A Saint Stephen limerick)
Our highways, frost-heaved, keep us hopping
To make it to town for some shopping.
    With their dips, dives and holes
    And while dodging the poles
We sometimes end up interlocking.
                    —*G. W. Jenkinson*

There once was a fellow named God,
Who created Man from a clod;
    Had He guessed the result,
    He'd have tried to consult
With a maker of better-class sod.
              —John Dunton

Haliburton, a writer of note,
On visiting Halifax, wrote:
    "Half the populace here
    Live by brewing of beer
(And the rest by the drinking, no doubt)."
              —M.I. Young

What wonderful stuff is this snow!
It comes when the North wind doth blow,
    Or South, West or East wind,
    Or even the least wind,
But when will the horrid stuff go?
              —H. Fred Bland

Smooth patches of ice on the street
Call for studious movement of feet.
    If you recklessly go
    On ice covered with snow,
You may land with a thud on your seat.
                    —*David Webster*

In Florida at Easter Newfs meet
While searching for sun, surf and heat.
    We leave here by the drove
    And I'll tell you, by Jove,
That this rock rises up by ten feet.
                    —*M. Knott*

A Micmac from Cape Breton Isle
Said with an ironic smile,
    "There's a few jobs for Macs
    But none for Micmacs —
I'd like to be Scots for a while."
                    —*Alan MacKenzie*

THE CONTEST, THE MAGAZINE AND THE LIMERICK FORM

Many contest entrants apparently
felt there might be a better chance
of winning if they mentioned in
their limerick the magazine or the
contest. Others celebrated the
limerick form itself.

Eaton's Catalogue has gone with no trace;
The privy seems not the same place.
    Oh, what to read
    When one feels the need?
Atlantic Insight quite fills the space.
                —*R. M. MacFie*

I don't have a flair for light versey,
But I do have some space in my pursey!
    With no money on hand,
    I'd think it quite grand,
If when judging you'd show me some mercy!
                    —*Edith Clouston*

Sometimes when I grow reflective
And wonder "What **is** life's objective?"
    I know wherever I roam,
    There's no other Down Home:
Insight helps keep my perspective.
                    —*R.M. MacFie*

There once was a writer named Bruce,
Who plucked several quills from a goose;
    New pens, now a-quiver
    His prose to deliver
In syntax connected, not loose.
                    —*Charles A. Crowell*

To write you one better—or worse,
And keep my verbosity terse,
　　My muse should perform
　　In a much better form:
Or be carried away...in a hearse!
　　　　　　　—*Eleanor Hankinson*

I wouldn't mind being immortal!
But I'm sure when I enter the portal,
　　And say "I can claim
　　The Great Limerick fame!"
St. Peter might stand there and chortle.
　　　　　　　—*Edith Clouston*

Ten years of *Atlantic Insight* —
Now the balance of content's just right;
　　Surette, Bruce and Ray
　　Each month "make my day" —
And my wife loves to read them at night.
　　　　　　　—*Edgar House*

There once was a writer named Guy —
He's really a Newfoundland boy.
   His wit it is sharp,
   He'll hoot and he'll harp
And slap 'em with pie in the eye.
               —*Jacqueline Barrett*

After ten years on tap, I still get
The best magazine I have seen yet.
   It's really great stuff,
   I can't get enough
Of Ray Guy, Harry Bruce and Surette.
               —*Ralph Martin*

For your contest, *Atlantic Insight*,
I respectfully submit, if I might,
   A limerick or two,
   And if they please you,
I'll win all the books with delight!
               —*R.J. "Buzz" Betts*

Some say that our limericks are crazy:
Just nonsense by those who are lazy
　　And don't wish to write
　　Other verses that might
Be more literate, metric and précis.
　　　　　　　　　—A. Reed Woory

Time hangs, and still people pick
The nasty, the noble lim'rick —
　　Two lines introduce,
　　Two tighten the noose,
Then the bottom drops out with a kick!
　　　　　　　　　—Jim Benjamin

But it's time to stop writing this stuff.
Anapestic-type rhyming gets tough.
　　It was fun at the start,
　　But it's starting to smart.
I'm no poet; it's all a big bluff.
　　　　　—Ken Dixon (final one of ten limericks)

PLACES

One of the most time-honoured
limerick techniques, of course, is
working the unexpected or unusual
rhyme with a place name.
Fortunately, this region has ample
place names suited to this purpose

At Quarryville, up near Renous,
There've been sightings of two kangaroos.
    They cause quite a fright
    When they come out at night
And nibble on poplar and spruce.
                    —*L. Gallant*

It's a wonderful day for a sail,
But, if you don't want to bail,
    You'd better not go
    Out beyond Baccaro
Where they say that it's blowing a gale.
                    —*Peter LeBlanc*

Goodbye, Nova Scotia! Farewell!
You have wonders the tongue cannot tell —
    Why, up in Baddeck
    There's a refugee Czech
Who dresses like Alex Graham Bell.
                    —*D. Theriault*

A gardner in Acadieville,
Using seeds bought from one Howard Dill,
   Grew a squash, which he found
   Weighed over six hundred pound,
And a zucchini that was heavier still.
                       —*Andy Vesey*

A lumbering man from Renous
Was chased up a tree by a moose.
   "Just as well," said the tree,
   "That you hadn't cut me,
If you see what I mean, *entre nous*."
                       —*George Peabody*

A luckless young man from St. Quentin
Came to visit his cousin in Benton.
   On the road past the dump,
   Hit a gigantic bump,
And drove out a lot worse than he went in.
                       —*John Green*

A Tyne Valley teacher one day
Thought, "This is not worth the pay;
   I'm tired and sick
   And bored to the quick.
I should be sailing in Cascumpec Bay."
                     —*Tim Reeves*

An earthquake up near Plaster Rock
Was a nasty though transient shock
   Causing landforms to quiver
   From Barnaby River
To the mouth of the Shigatehawk.
                   —*George Peabody*

A girl from the Eastern Shore
Said, "Even though life is a bore,
   I know it would be dumb
   To leave Ecum Secum,
But I hate to stay here even more!"
                   —*L. Boutilier*

A chef down in Dartmouth, N.S.,
By mistake in a moment of stress,
   Stirred baking powder
   Into his clam chowder
Where it fizzed in a horrible mess!
        —H. MacPhee

A Rogersville farmer said, "See,
I told you the bank would agree.
    There's no room for doubts
    That more Brussels sprouts
Are the wave of the future for me."
                    —*Dave Richard*

In the village of Indian Harbour,
There once lived a rather odd barber.
    It was considered a treat
    To watch him shave with his feet
In the shade of a homemade grape arbour.
                    —*Lynn Graham*

A Lower Economy lass
Said, "The Church is the place for stained
glass.
    In secular pieces
    My interest decreases.
I find them both tacky and crass."
                    —*Judy Robichaud*

For sheer geographic deceit,
Halifax is sure hard to beat:
    Who would have guessed
    Streets named *North* and *West*
Would run parallel to *South* Street?
             —*Lloyd Smith*

To a bog near St-Louis-de-Kent,
An anchorite frequently went.
    He fasted and prayed
    And sometimes he stayed,
But he only lived there during Lent.
             —*George Peabody*

St. Stephen's the sweetest small town
You can find anywhere all around.
    The folks there make money
    From chocolate not honey,
Selling chicken bones by the pound.
             —*T.J. Nason*

A restaurant employee from Cape Sable
Got tired of waiting on tables.
    After thinking a while,
    She took a flight to the Isle
And tried out for Anne of Green Gables.
                            —*J. Nickerson*

A world-weary Malpeque Bay oyster
Was sent to the calm of a cloister,
    Where a Carmelite nun
    Ate him, fried, on a bun,
Then remarked, "You know, raw, they're
much moister."
                            —*George Peabody*

At Goobies, or somewhere up there,
A man who was devil-may-care
    Walked from Argentia
    Halfway to Placentia
And back again, just on a dare.
                            —*Sam MacKinnon*

A musical woman named Fay
Found city life rather outré.
   In a small fit of pique,
   She moved back to Judique
Where she plays on the bagpipes all day.
     —*Kay MacDonald*

When ya live in the town of Tignish
Where there's not much ta do but ta fish,
    Ya rock and ya search
    Fer yer fun and yer work,
And ya curse and ya pray and ya wish...
              —Jim Benjamin

In P.E.I., N.S., N.B.
It's friendly and (ha ha) carefree —
    In p.m. or a.m.
    There's never much mayhem,
P.S. (and in NFLD!)
              —Jim Benjamin

A feisty young man from Calais
On Sunday partook of the chalice.
    On weekdays he swore,
    Drank, gambled and more,
But on Sabbath God bore him no malice.
           —Alex Merrill

A fellow at work in Bear River
Was pierced by one helluva sliver.
   The nurse said, "Oh dear,
   This will hurt you, I fear;
Count three, grit your teeth, then I'll give 'er!"
          —*Jonathan Hilton*

A preacher from Ingonish Beach
Gave a powerful anti-booze speech.
   He prepared for the task
   By upending a flask
Of one-hundred proof Newfoundland Screech.
          —*George Sutherland*

A P.E.I. tourist, Buchanan,
Never finished his holiday plannin'.
   He quite lost his mind
   Whilst trying to find
Upper Old Lower New Annan.
          —*George Sutherland*

There once was a man from Glace Bay
Who, in a lighthearted way,
    Went to Whitney Pier
    For a couple of beer
And did not get home 'til next day.
                —*Bill MacDonald*

There once was a handsome young he-gull
Fell in love with a beautiful she-gull.
    They were wed on a wave
    Near the Isle of LaHave,
By the minister, Reverend E. Gull.
           —*Peggy Hopper, Joanne Jefferson,*
                  Stephen Jefferson

There was a young lady of Milton
Who posed, for a lark, with her kilt on.
  When they said "Will you smile?"
  She said "Yes, in a while,
But only if I can say 'Stilton.'"
                              —K.M. West

A professional seer from Kileerly,
Who prized his profession quite dearly,
  Once said, with a grin,
  "Whenever I sin,
I try awfully hard to sin seerly."
                              —Lorne Gardiner
                *(who notes bilingually: "If there is no
                Kileerly in Atlantic Canada, there damn
                well should be; or/ou, si Kileerly
                n'existait pas, il faudrait l'inventer.")*

A half-witted fellow from Guelph,
Half-dying because of ill-health,
  On his half-holiday,
  Got half-drunk, so they say,
And a monocle made of himself.
                              —George Brodie

There once was a man from N.S.
Who said "Things out west are a mess.
    Me for NFLD.,
    P.E.I. or N.B.,
Or back to good old Inverness."
                              —*E.A. Neilson*

There was a young girl from Cape Ray
Who was rowing a punt on the bay.
    She got a shocking surprise,
    When before her young eyes
Two humpbacks were humping away!
                        —*Joseph B. Ruttgaizer*

REGIONAL PRIDE

A number of contestants tried to
wax eloquent about the charms and
characteristics of the region,
although the limerick is not a
forgiving form for attempting this

How we do love our Atlantic coast!
Of fishing and farming we boast.
  Our people are workers;
    Not patient with shirkers.
Maritimers! We are the most!
                    —Mrs. Evelyne Day

There once was a time that young men
Could stay with their Atlantic kin,
    But as you may know,
    I'm in high Arctic snow
Wishing I were back home again.
                    —Kevin Michael Kelly

I wish I could fly through the air
With great speed so I could be there
    To stroll through the grasses,
    Or eat golden molasses,
(Or some other fine Maritime fare.)
                    —Elizabeth Courneya

Most Ontario natives I know
Say "Down East is a great place to go
     For a visit," they say,
     "But it's no place to stay."
Which shows just how little they know.

                    —R.J. "Buzz" Betts

FISHING

A short category, but with
considerable importance, fishing
being, after all, a regional
preoccupation

My Acadian brother-in-law
Caught a lobster with one extra claw.
   He measured and weighed it,
   And briefly displayed it,
Then served it with new *petit pois.*
               —*Eric Stephen*

Weary of living afloat,
A fisherman sold off his boat
   And moved in great style
   To a house in Argyle
With six cats, two dogs and a goat.
               —*Hugh MacLeod*

"There's billions of cod off our coasts,"
A Newfoundland fisherman boasts,
   "But if the French aren't restricted,
   'Tis easily predicted
There'll be nothing out there but cod-ghosts."
               —*Paul Whalen*

Near Belledune on Baie des Chaleurs,
There used to be fishing, *bien sur*.
   But nowdays, they say
   There's things in the bay
That shouldn't be brought up on shore.
          —*R. Joseph*

There once was a man who caught cod,
Who asked when he died that his bod
   Be dropped in the sea
   Where he wanted to be
'Cause he had not a love for the sod.
          —*Pamela Hurley*

CULTURE SHOCK

People in the region are always
fascinated by the doings of those
well-known "come-from-aways."

A back-to-the-land refugee
After fifteen years in N.B.
 Said, "I'm so weary
 Of living in Geary,
I think I'll move out to B.C."
     —*Stephanie Clarke*

At Frizzleton near Margaree,
A newcomer suffered ennui.
 He said that the locals
 Were nothing but yokels
And thought it the best way to be!
     —*A.K. MacDonald*

A Buddhist who came from away
Ate bananas in a state of decay.
 He found them erotic
 And macrobiotic
Though no one could think them gourmet.
     —*George Peabody*

A come-from-away in Tignish
Said "You know, I really do wish
    There'd be occasional talk
    Of Shakespeare or Bach,
But here they think mostly of fish."
                    —*George Peabody*

Laid back in the land of red soil,
With a pot full o' lobsters on boil,
    It's hard not to pity
    The poor rich in the city
As they race to unwrap their tinfoil.
                    —*Jim Benjamin*

TOURISM

Sometimes the "come-from-aways"
don't stay very long, but they are a
rich source of entertainment
nonetheless.

It's flat on the Isle of Miscou,
And there's nothing to ruin the view;
    It's a fine place to rest,
    And watch the birds nest,
But there sure isn't much else to do!
              —*Alain Lemaire*

Some tourists come here to hunt;
Others place fishing up front.
    But they all want to know
    If in August there's snow,
And what makes our blueberries grunt.
              —*J. C Thompson*

In Saint John, the Reversing Falls
Is the most liked of all tourist calls.
    The tide and the foam
    Are like nothing back home.
It's only the smell that appalls.
              —*Dave Irving*

If glass buildings give you a thrill,
Then welcome to Halifax. Still,
    All those bank towers
    Mean you can't see the hours
On the clock on Citadel Hill.
                  —Joan Smith

At Chatham Head, Miramichi,
There really is not much to see.
    Don't stop for the view,
    Just drive right on through
The way tourists all do in N.B.
                  —Susan Kelly

There's tourists from far and from near
Who visit the Island each year.
    It's no act of God;
    Thank Saint Lucy Maud
For setting Anne of Green Gables down here.
                  —Marie Boudreau

They hang out in Halifax bars,
Snap photos of *Bluenose II*'s spars,
    But come fall they'll all go
    Back to On-tar-i-o,
With lobster traps lashed to their cars.
                    —*George Peabody*

If Peggy still owned Peggy's Cove,
Where tourists arrive by the drove,
     She'd offer a thank,
     Drive her Rolls to the bank —
She'd be richer than Midas or Jove.
                    —*Tom Vail*

A tourist from somewhere Down East,
Said "It may be a Grand Manan feast,
     But I think you'll convulse
     If you eat that much dulse:
It's a pound-and-a-half, at the least!"
                    —*George Peabody*

A tourist who had searched far and wide
For a really magnificent tide
     Said, "The best is on Fundy
     On a warm sunny Sunday
As you wait for the clams to be fried."
                    —*Mrs. E. Courneya*

A LIMERICK HISTORY OF HALIFAX

A contributor who used limericks
as components of a larger verse
undertook an epic! In his covering
letter, which also included a
limerick, Paul Gouett described
himself tongue-in-cheek as the
"ghost writer" of his submission on
the grounds that the original teller
of the tale was dead and Gouett
had heard it at a seance...

Jolly Jack Tar of the Eastern Star
(A Limerick History of Halifax)

'Round this heavenly Ale House we're sailors,
The spirits of pirates and whalers.
   Some's rogues indiscreet,
   Some be men of the fleet,
Some were fishers, some press men, some bailers.

Some have rounded the Horn 'n' tell stories
O' their shipwrecks, o' battles 'n' glories.
   Some worked freighters 'n' sinned,
   Some have sailed on the wind,
Some worked frigates ur liners; some dories.

But none hold a candle, I'm sayin'
To the ghost o' one sailor for 'splayin':
   He's called Jolly Jack Tar
   From the old *Eastern Star* —
That's of Halifax town, I'm a' prayin'.

Now before I goes inta this story,
I'll assure ya 'tis naught that'll bore ye;
   'Tis all sober true —
   From me cap ta me shoe.
'Tis made up uv 'is lore and 'is glory.

On one day 'e strode into this tavern,
Makin' straight fer the stern o' the cavern.
   'E be such a big lug
   Wit' a fierce lookin' mug,
That there weren't not a sound from the
brethren.

'E be such a great hulk that we listened,
Drank 'is health 'fore the story be christened.
    Then 'e sets down 'is mug
    After taking a slug,
Sized us up wit' 'is dark eyes what glistened.

To the bar 'e then made with a swagger,
'N' his voice cut the air like a dagger,
    "Don't be fearin' o' me,
    I'se a man o' the sea
With a story ta tell 'fore I stagger."

"Gather round all ye mates fer my story —
'Tis of Halifax town and 'er glory.
    Put yer ears on me chat
    Let yer grog go all flat,
Else I'll set ye adrift in a dory."

Then 'e pulls out a map from 'is boot top,
'Twas right dirty 'n' worn like a deck mop,
    'E then spreads 'er out free
    So's each man could see,
And stood silent so you'd hear a pin drop.

So…the land mass 'twere all Nova Scotian
From Chignecto right through ta the ocean.
    Then his finger 'e jabbed
    Through the air as 'e stabbed
It at Halifax, all in one motion.

"This 'ere town be the spot fer my tellin';
'Tis 'er legends and lore I'm a-sellin'.
    So jist listen right close
    Ta this tale o' the coast,
'Tis all true, and the facts I'se not swellin'.

All the souls 'ere was once called "colonial",
But that were all full a' "bolonial".
    They ain't dumb, they's right rum,
    They's not folks on the bum,
They's the "Indigo Proboscolonials"!

We built up this place from the forest,
Behind the brave Edward Cornwallis.
    It were quite a rough job,
    But we was a strong mob,
'Sides, an easy time woulda jist bored us.

I won't act like an iggorant blaggard,
Er speak of my town like a braggard
    I'll give ye a sketch,
    'N from mem'ry I'll fetch
Some old tales that'll make ye be staggered.

Long before young Cornwallis did land 'ere,
Chebucto'd been earmarked: "Expand 'ere!" —
    The Frenchmen 'ad tried
    But their fleet'd all died,
So the spark uv'r growth, it weren't fanned'ere.

Then next came this mighty big treaty,
'Tween England 'n' France (it be meaty!) —
    Utrecht it be called,
    And the English be lolled
Inta thinkin' it be quite a sweetie.

But at Louisbourg soon they saw clearly
That France were not actin' sincerely.
    The build-up uv their might
    Now tossed England a fright
By their threat'nin' to treat 'em undearly.

I'll not ruin this tale by expandin'
On how Louisbourg fell from our plannin'.
    We dismantled their fort,
    Wrecked some houses for sport,
And made sure not a wall was left standin'.

Now we needed a mighty fine 'arbour
To protect all the spoils of our ardour.
    Chebucto was great
    With its nachural-made shape,
But we had to work faster and harder.

Quite soon we built wharves and defences,
The palisades, cannons and fences.
    With growth in 'er trade,
    She'd 'er destiny made
As a seaport of note and dimensions.

In wartimes there came some strong fellows,
The cat o' nine, press gang, and gallows.
    I recalls I drank swill
    Up on Citadel Hill
Just to block out the fear of them callows.

Then the Citadel Hill, I'm a-tellin'
Was right ringed by the whores and the felons,
    So her fringes was rough
    'Cause they housed mainly scruff,
With 'er rum shops 'n' gutters all smellin'.

She be quite a tough town fer us sailors,
But just like 'er merchants or tailors,
    We loved 'er right well,
    But I'm here fer ta tell,
That I don't care a bit fer 'er jailors.

With fishin' boats, navy and traders,
And soldier boys all in their gaiters,
    The town was right full,
    So she was never dull,
With her fighters, her girls and debators.

But worst was the Narrows' Explosion,
It wrecked the town right ta the ocean.
    With some hundreds left dead
    And the town filled with dread,
It was strewn with a pall of emotion.

In the Second World War 'twere amazin'
How the times brought a sharp end to lazin':
    All the convoys 'ud group
    Just as thick as pea soup
Then fer Murmansk 'r Britain go racin'.

But I'd best not drag on 'cause I'm fearin'
Me eyeballs will soon take ta blearin'.
    'Tis not 'cause I'm sad —
    Ye might say that I'm glad
I had something ta do with 'er rearin'.

'Cause we built up this town, I'm a-sayin',
She's a fine one and well worth displayin'.
    So I'm right proud, of course,
    From the Arm to the wharf,
And she'll prosper and grow, I'm a-prayin'.

So raise up yer mugs ta this city,
And ta Halifax girls what's so pretty.
    Now drink yer mugs down
    To this Halifax town
And the end of this Sailor Jack's ditty."

Tho' old Jolly Jack Tar now were finished,
Yet his presence still grew not diminished.
    Fer us sailors now knew
    That the legend were true,
An' we'd just heard 'er told quite unblemished.

Fer men told 'round tables held speechless,
Of one whose brave deeds was impeachless.
    His name be Jack Tar
    And his face has a scar
That disfigured 'is weatherworn features.

Then 'e spoke one more time to us masses
His words coming slow as molasses.
    "If I'm lyin', ye think,
    Then, 'tis into the drink
That I'll kick ye, for bein' such asses!"

But we all knew his story were crystal,
She be knowed from New Bedford to Bristol.
    No one doubted 'is word,
    As we all had once heard
That this man was as clean as a whistle.

Now this legend were 'ere in our presence,
Before 'im we all seemed like peasants.
    We all knew uv 'is fame
    And we'd all heard the name
Of this man who'd made Halifax crescent.
                 —Paul Gouett

ENVIRONMENT AND NATURE

The budworm's killed many a tree,
But now they've declared it to be
    By order of law
    A new tourist draw:
The provincial insect of N.B.
                    —*J. Underhill*

Halifax has its Citadel Hill
Overlooking a scenic hog swill.
    It must be that way
    The town fathers say
Since thereby we're saved a big bill.
                    —*Mildred Burrows*

Once Halifax Harbour was clean
With water a translucent green,
    Then Man had a notion:
    Sewage goes in the ocean.
Now pollution is spoiling the scene.
                    —*E. Mosher*

The environment's falling apart:
Take PCB's or CFC's for a start —
    Then there's Greenhouse Effects,
    Acid rain...what comes next?
Doesn't sound like we're acting too smart.
                    —*Karen MacInnes*

At Blue Mountain, the people all say
"Log off that hillside? No way!
    We'll force them to stop,
    For they think it's a crop,
And they'll cut down the trees just like hay!"
                    —*Tim Kennedy*

They're burning the dump in Grand Bay.
You can smell it from three miles away.
    The fumes are obnoxious
    And probably toxious.
Why can't they just let it decay?
                    —*Neil Kirkpatrick*

There was a young man from Port Hope
Who coated his palate with soap,
   Thus disguising the taste
   Of the nuclear waste
With which he no longer could cope.
              —*Edward Baxter*

The harbour is really a sewer;
The water is very impure.
   It's stagnant by light,
   Gives tourists a fright,
And has a bouquet like day-old manure.
              —*David Perry*

The value of your average newt
To most people seems rather moot.
   But the newt has a niche
   In the life of a witch,
And an eye for a potion, to boot!
              —*Jim Benjamin*

A professor of bugdom has stated,
"The June Bug is way under-rated.
 Though it's ugly and blind
 With no measurable mind,
Obviously, many have mated!"
—*Judy Bourque*

We once had some skunks on our lawn;
They stayed there from midnight to dawn.
 They dug up the slugs
 And ate all the bugs,
But now our green grass is all gone!
—*Edna MacLeod*

SPORTS

A hopelessly cornered, brave pheasant
Said "To hunters and everyone present —
    I'm tasty, I know,
    And a sport, even so,
To me, this is damn-well unpleasant!"
           —*Jim Benjamin*

There once was a runner named Ben
Who won prizes and medals and then,
    With drugs anabolic
    He went on a frolic
Which brought his career to an end.
           —*Dave Hingley*

When "birdie" begins with a "tee,"
It's a Bore with a capital B!
    It's pleasant to play
    On a green sunny day,
But who can watch golf on TV?
              —*Jim Benjamin*

Football fanatics have fun
Yelling "Blitz 'im!" and "Pass it!" and "Run!"
    They howl when they see
    A T.D. on T.V.
And their jowls move more than their buns.
              —*Jim Benjamin*

OF SCANDALS, LOVE AFFAIRS, BEES, AND CLOVER

In the year that they built Halifax
A Lady, who'd gone home to relax,
    Became embroiled in a scandal
    With George Frederick Handel
And a Frenchman who played on the sax.
              —Tom Bradey

This summer has not been a breeze:
The ragweed has made us all sneeze,
    While most of the beaches
    Are infested with leeches
And the wood ticks all spread Lyme Disease.
              —Susan Adams

At an auction, my Aunt Edna bought
A painting, as part of a lot.
    It was marked 'Anonymous,'
    But I think it's by Hieronymus
Bosch. Does she know what she's got?
              —Lynn Jones

A bartender out in Cape Broyle
Mixes drinks from which many recoil:
   He shakes up some Screech
   With white sand from the beach
And two jiggers of cod liver oil.
          —*L. Winsor*

Your cat is not supposed to be
Climbing up in our catalpa tree!
    There's a bird's nest up there,
    And I'm giving you fair
Warning of cat-astrophe!
                    —Ellen Smith

A man on his way to make merry
Crossed on the Halifax ferry
    Clad only in socks
    Of green and white blocks
And a chapeau of bright purple terry!
              —Mrs. Clare MacDormand

There was a young woman named Fay,
Who, early one morning in May,
    Woke up in bed
    To find that her head
Had somehow been taken away!
               —Michael Daigle

There once was a dimwit named Zorro,
Who thought there was always tomorrow.
    Used a match to test gas:
    That was rash—so, alas!
For Zorro there was no tomorrow.
                  —Mary S. Horne

I have walked a great many miles
To deliver some chuckles and smiles.
    Sometimes to resentment,
    At others, contentment,
But at least I have my own styles.
                 —James J. Hewitt

Have you considered the merits of books?
Their contents, their authors, their looks...
    They are better, you see
    Than radio or T.V.;
And you can store them on shelves or in
nooks.
                 —Cecilia MacIsaac

I'd like to fill a volume with verse
Before I'm taken away in a hearse:
    It's not the work that I mind,
    It's trying to find
Inspiration to do it that's worse!
             —*Edward W. Britt*

(This one only works with the author's
explanation that "Patty graduated an
audiologist and soon after got married.")

There once was a lassie named Patty —
That girl drove her poor parents batty;
    She studied for years
    To learn about ears,
And graduated, summa cum laddie!
             —*Danielle MacAulay Williams*

A Bumblebee fuddled by bee balm
Thought to himself "If I stay calm,
    And hang on this flower
    For another half-hour
I'll get airborne on two wings and a psalm."
             —*T. Lutes*

They've found the *Titanic* at last;
She's a gruesome glimpse of the past.
    Down there in the deep
    Where crawly things creep,
Do her flags still fly at half-mast?
                    —*John L. MacDonald*

I have a wee friend name of Molly;
She visits along with her dolly.
    When we're ready to eat,
    She asks "What's the treat?"
I say "Kentucky Fried Chicken, by golly!"
                    —*Mrs. Morris Higgins*

There once was a tiger named Tony
Who admitted to being a phony —
    "My teeth ain't my own,
    My muscles are foam,
And I roar with the help of a Sony."
                    —*Jim Benjamin*

Barbershopping's a high-level art
From the tenors down to the bass part,
    And the people who sing it
    Will often just wing it
And belt it out straight from the heart.
                    —*David Perry*

I once knew a blind man named Nick
Who constantly walked with a stick;
    He found his way round
    By prodding the ground,
And what didn't bark, he would kick.
                    —*Laura Morry Williams*

He said "She'll do ninety or over!"
As he raced down the road in his Rover
    When he hit ninety-five,
    He went into a dive
And now he is pushing up clover.
                    —*Mildred Shannon*

A pretentious young man of great style
Lost the better part of his smile,
    When the car that he bought
    Fell apart from dry rot,
And lay in the road in a pile!
                    —*Daniel O'Brien*

My books were returned late today.
The librarian said "You must pay!"
   "I will take out a loan,"
   I said with a groan —
"Fine with me," was all she would say.
                 —*Linda Durling*

I once had a girl, Guinivere,
Whose exploits I won't relate here,
   Except for to say
   That in only one day
She could spend what I make in a year.
                 —*A.M. Fraser*

I'm a perfectionist and I admit it.
When I see the infinitive split, it
   Gives me pain to behold,
   But before I'm too old,
I hope to eventually quit it!
                 —*A. M. Fraser*

At the launch of the ship *Marco Polo*,
A pessimist warned it would go slow.
   He said "Mark my words —
   No firsts, seconds, thirds:
She'll never win fame, that I do know."
                 —*A. L. Martin*

When Blanchards or Comeaus get the yen
To find out about life way back when,
   They can see it all
   From Spring until Fall
At le Village Acadien.
                 —*Peter Comeau*

A Newfoundland soldier named Fred,
Who was constantly wetting his bed,
   Said "By the Lard Garge,
   When I gets me discharge,
I'll piss in the Sergeant's, instead!"
                 —*C.M. Ogilvie*

A pretty young thing was demanding
Proper marriage with him she was landing.
    But he said "That won't do,
    Because married to you,
I'd be losing my amateur standing."
                 —*Mabel B. Smythe*

There once was a minister's daughter
Who didn't do all that she oughta
    When out on a date
    She came home too late,
Having forgot what her father had taught her.
              — *Elsie M. Kirk*